I would like to dedicate this book to my amazing wife who made me see that anything is possible in life.

Unstoppable Life Now:

Goals

How to make yourself unstoppable and your goals inevitable without self-discipline or will-power.

By Paul Shepherd

Dear Reader,

Thank you for choosing my book. Thanks for putting your faith in me. I am grateful. I hope I can help you. I believe I can help you change your life.

If you have some free time, send me an email telling me what you would like to read about in a forthcoming book.

If you would like more information sign up at my website unstoppablelifenow.com. You will occaisionally get an update with the news about any forthcoming books and products.

If you have any questions or feedback, don't hesitate to contact me at paul@unstoppablelifenow.com. Also if there are any errors, please contact me.

Once again, many thanks. It is my duty to ensure that you won't regret it.

Paul Shepherd

INTRODUCTION

Thank you for choosing to read this book. I hope it inspires you to change what you want to change in your life. There are over 100 exercises in this book. If you do them all, I'm 100% certain it will.

In my life I have read so many books on self-help, psychology, and philosophy. I spent 5 years studying philosophy at college and university. So I have tried to distill my knowledge into this book and I know at least one thing, that if applied consistently, will change your life radically.

You may choose just one thing to change, or everything, but I'm confident you will because these thoughts and techniques have changed me.

Have you ever had a conversation like this:

"Just do it."

"What do you mean 'just do it'"?

"What are you waiting for?"

"Not now. Maybe later"

"Why not now?"

"I'll explain later"

"You never do!"

I have. I'm sure that if you are reading this, then you might have too, or you are reading this to help someone you care dearly for. Well, I hope you have finally found the way to free yourself, or your loved one or friend. I really want to help you because, yes, I have been there.

I always felt I was destined for greatness. I was going to be the new Tolstoy, or Dickens, or Hemingway! And then the new Bill Gates, Warren Buffet, Richard Branson! There's nothing wrong in aspiring to be the best in what you love to do. We would never have witnessed the brilliant and fantastic sporting achievements of the greatest athletes had they never aspired to be the greatest. But the greatest procrastinator? Sadly, for me, there are no gold medals and sponsorship deals for procrastination.

Maybe you know a greater procrastinator than me? People don't tend to advertise that they just can't get over their procrastination. Maybe my procrastination is nothing compared to others, and I would use that reason to procrastinate a little more. It may be true that there are greater procrastinators, but when I wanted it to end, and just get simple things done, it really did feel like I was the greatest procrastinator.

I would delay doing simple things like washing the dishes, having a shave, having a head shave (yes I have very little hair), emptying the bins. But I also delayed some really important things too. I waited until I was 38 before I had my first serious relationship. (No, no, I know what you may be thinking, I had some short-term relationships.) I was never ready. I was too fat. I was too boring. I'm not very romantic. Why would anyone like me? Excuse after excuse by my so-called friend: my brain. "I'll just wait a little longer before I quit my job. Maybe next month will be different." It wasn't. It was I who had to be different. "I'll continue for years with this business that barely makes enough for us to survive." I had to stop. Enough. No more.

I was tired of waiting for things to happen. I was tired of never feeling fulfilled. I was tired of never having real love. I was just sick and tired of it all. So I eventually did meet the woman of my dreams. Married after 1 year together. "Well if you don't know now, when will you know?" was what my wife said at the time. I guess she was right. That's not to say marriage is what everyone should do, if that's not part of a person's life goals, but if you aspire to it, and if you are certain that you're with the right person, get on with it. Maybe it will be a success, maybe it will a failure. No-one can predict the future, and people change with time. "I can't right now" "Why not now?" Ah yes. The procrastination. Sorry.

I have to give my all to help you solve your problem quickly. Sometimes when you do whatever it takes to help someone, you create an unbreakable and unforgettable bond between each other, even though we may never meet.

So I am going to help you act when you want and how you want, and nothing and no-one will be able to stop you. I want you to have to the freedom to act when you please. I want to help you get closer to the greatest version of yourself. Maybe there will be a time like me when you remember your old self. I'm nowhere near being the greatest version of myself, and I have no doubt, you could teach me a lot too. Let's move forward together. Let's not let anything stop us.

What you will learn in this book:

1. That it's not unusual to be tired of trying to change your life.
2. That perhaps you really don't want to change.
3. What you must believe in order to change.
4. That your current life can not go on as it is.
5. A method for change.
6. There is no such thing as a difficult goal.
7. Neither positivity nor negativity are best.
8. You are closer to change than you think.
9. Why self-discipline doesn't work.
10. Why will-power is unnecessary.
11. That your brain is not really your friend or your enemy.
12. About the power of words.
13. What the formula for change is.
14. Why you will become obsessed.

There are exercises at the end of each chapter, and an additional 75 exercises at the end of the book. You may choose do them as you read the book or after you have read the whole book. You may choose do as many as you like. The more exercises you do, the more effective this book will be in helping you.

Key Points

1. Repetition is the mother of success.
2. I know of one thing that if applied consistently will change your life radically.
3. Do you feel destined for greatness?
4. Do you procrastinate about doing simple things?
5. Are you tired of waiting for things to happen?
6. Do you want to act when you want and how you want?

Exercises

1. Have you ever just kept delaying doing something?

Try to remember a time in your life when you just kept putting things off. Or it could just be something that you just can't get yourself to do. Don't worry if you can't think of anything at the moment. If you're like me you'll probably remember when doing something else entirely. Write it down.

2. Do you believe that life could be so much better than now?

Take a look at your life now. Do you think it could be much better? If your lucky enough to have a great life, I congratulate you. This book will still be useful to you. However if you don't, I'm sure I can help. So do you wonder why you just can't get life to change for the better? Write down how you feel about life at the moment.

3. Do you believe that you are just as good as other people, but you just don't know how to succeed?

Do you really believe that you are stupider than other people? You're not. I wish I could tell you in person that you're not. You just need new techniques. You just haven't been taught correctly. So repeat to yourself for five minutes. "I am just as good as everyone else."

CHAPTER 1. TIRED OF TRYING

Are you tired of trying to improve your life? Nothing seems to be working? That's how it feels to me sometimes. But that's not how it feels most of the time now. And that's what's the goal should be. If you are trying to be perfect in all areas at the same time, then it's really going to be a struggle. And I'll tell you a secret that you probably already suspect. There will never be a time when it's perfect. There will only be times when life is better or worse. Some may feel sad at the idea. But I don't see it that way.

Have you ever seen your team win a sporting championship? Have you ever won a prize? Or have you ever bought something after waiting months and months and months? It's great, for about a day, then it begins not to seem so great, and then its just normal. You bought the car you really wanted, and you love driving it, and then with time, it's just normal. It eventually gets a little boring to drive around in. You want something new. The car hasn't changed. It's a bit older. It's you who's changed.

So even if you keep trying to change, when you do change, you'll eventually want to change again. So what's the point? Why even change? That's a good question. Shouldn't we all just be satisfied with what we have? Maybe. But that's not what you really want. You've seen others with more than you and your family. You want the best for your family. You're tired of trying and failing. Or worse, you don't know how to begin. You're tired of wanting life to be different, but you feel helpless and hopeless. Maybe I'm wrong.

But I don't think so. No-one likes to admit that life is not doing too well. We put on a brave face. We get up everyday. We do our best. And nevertheless, life just doesn't seem to go anywhere. I know the feeling. At times we ignore it, at others times we rage against it, at times we cry about it. I have too. No more. No more! It strains relationships. It upsets the people we love. The phrase: "Life sucks!" often feels very very true. Sometimes we just want life to suck less.

Of course, it's possible. We see it all around us. People living what appear to be better lives. If they can live like that, why can't we? You know it's possible. My goal is to make you see that it's probable, and then eventually inevitable. I know you sometimes feel like giving up and just accepting life as it is. You think there must be some secret that other people know that you don't. Or that they are sell-outs, corrupt, liars, or whatever. Or you may think it's a conspiracy against you, or the ordinary person by big business, the government, foreign powers, aliens, whatever. That's the easy answer. It's not the answer that you must face up to.

You are just not good enough right now. You're just not good enough right now in an area of your life that you want to change. You need to face up to that right now. Accept it. Accept it. Denial will only stop you. When you accept it, you can begin to change it. With anger, with passion, with drive, with love, with self-love, you can change it. You can be great at whatever you want to do. You can even the best that ever lived in what you want to do.

You must believe that you yourself are in an unacceptable situation right now. If you think it's not so bad, then you won't change. If you believe the situation is unacceptable, you'll do everything to get out of the situation.

You are tired of trying, but you must also become tired of this unacceptable situation. It may not be so serious. You may simply want to learn a new language, and currently you don't know it. You want to change and become fluent in a language but you can't seem to get the hang of it. You could give up. That's one way out of the unacceptable situation. Or you could do whatever it takes to become fluent. But the most important thing is that you control what you do.

You are responsible for your life. Up until we are 18, others are responsible for us. After that you are responsible for your actions, and the consequences of your actions. We've all made mistakes, and sometimes really big mistakes, but accept them, learn from them, and move on.

"But I just can't get over it".

You may have the luxury of wallowing in the thoughts about your mistake, but others don't. Your loved ones can't wait. Stand up. I know you can be the greatest at whatever you want to be.

It won't be easy, it may take years, but it's not as hard as you think. You are on the path to a new life already. It may not seem that way, but I can see we are on the same road. We can do it, I know we can. Trust me. I want you to know that I believe in you. You may have no-one else. But I will always believe that you can have the life you want. Why? Because you're human just like me. And if I know I can have the life I want, then so can you. It may even be easier and faster for you than me.

So it's time to stop being tired of trying. In fact the time of trying and struggling is over. It's time to change.

Key Points

1. It's not unusual to be tired of trying to improve your life.
2. We often change our attitude to something we really hoped for.
3. We want the best for ourselves and those we care about.
4. We put on a brave face even though we really want life to be much better.
5. We need to face up to the truth.
6. You're just not good enough right now in an area of your life that you want to change.
7. You must believe you are in an unacceptable situation right now.
8. You are in control of what you do.
9. You are responsible for your life.
10. You can not have the luxury of wallowing in the thoughts about your mistakes.

Exercises

1. What are you sick and tired of trying to do?

Write down what you are just tired of trying to do. For me it was my weight and trying to lose it. It could be that you want to earn more money. It could be that you're in a lousy relationship that doesn't seem to change no matter how hard you try. It could be that you never meet the right people when dating. It could be that your business isn't growing like you want it to.

2. Who is responsible for your life being the way it is?

Write down whatever and whoever is to blame. From childhood to now. Of course some people are to blame. It's not all your choice how people acted towards you. In many cases, it has nothing to do with you as to why some people did what they did. They're just malicious. It's your choice what to do about it. Fundamentally, you are much stronger than they. You just need to know how to call it forth.

3. Repeat the following for at least five minutes for each of the things you want to change. If it is more than three, pick the most important three things and just focus on those for now.

"No more <insert whatever you are sick and tired of>. No more!"

For example:

"No more being fat. No more!"
"No more being single. No more!"
"No more being unable to increase sales by two percent. No more!"

Perhaps not the last one. Make sure it is short and to the point.

"No more low sales. No more!"

The more you do this the more power it will have

CHAPTER 2. DO YOU REALLY WANT TO CHANGE?

Do you want to change? Maybe you don't.

"Of course I do, that's why I'm reading this!"

How much do you want to change? Just a little, then it's not going to work. If you've not cried, or shouted at yourself, or felt that deep fear inside of you of being on the verge of living on the street, then maybe you really don't want to change. Maybe you just think it would be kind of nice to change. I can buy a new car. I can buy a new house. I'll have some savings. But I'm not too bothered.

Well, it's not impossible, but it won't be as easy as someone else. If you feel like you are going to be living on the street, or feel like you are going to be very sick if you don't change, you'll change much easier. But don't worry. We can create the emotional intensity to change. You may not like the way you feel when it occurs, but that's good. You never ever want to feel like that unless you absolutely have to. And I'll tell you a little secret. You absolutely have to if you want to change quickly. Sorry. But then you will change, and you will feel amazing.

I can only guarantee two things when it comes to change. If you don't try, you won't change. And if you try the same thing, you will get the same result. Of course, you and I try. We've tried many times. We want to change, but nothing seems to work. We learn a new way to manage our time, or to run faster, or to clean a piece of old brass, and yet what we do doesn't work too well. It's just average. It's not so bad. We have a new piece of information. We adjust the method a little, and then it's more effective.

"But it seems so slow."

Yes I know, but it's progress. It's moving forward by a step, and it may seem like a step in the wrong direction. It's seems that way, but there aren't really steps in the wrong direction. There are just alternative routes to the right direction. Some people can swim easily after 20 minutes of instruction, others struggle for days. Either way it's movement in the right way and you may feel a lot of pain and heartache before you realize that something has to change. And if you feel horrified at the thought of not changing, you will be on the fast lane to change.

At least you are trying, and eventually you will tire of trying. You'll believe all sort of incorrect notions about yourself and your capabilities. And I'll tell you one thing I know about you even though we've never met. You don't know the full extent of your capabilities.

You have an idea. But it's not correct. More on that later.

And then, there are some who do the same thing, day in and day out, and expect a different result. They're trying too, but they are just doing the same thing over and over again. They keep banging on the floor, and wondering why they can't be heard in China. These are the people who don't believe the evidence of their own senses. These are the people who don't understand what they are looking for. They don't know what correct should look like. And I was one of those people, and in some situations, I'm still that person, until I get my head straight.

Or even worse, they keep doing the same thing over and over again, they ignore the results of their actions, and then complain that nothing changes. For example, they keep driving down the same traffic filled road, and complain that there's too much traffic. Maybe turn down a side road? I don't know about you, but I double-take when I talk to people like this. I get extraordinarily frustrated with them.

So, I'll ask the question again: Do you really want to change? Will you accept that maybe, just maybe, you really are not that bothered about changing? Or that you really don't want to change, but you don't see any other alternative? You wish you could have the same life as now but with different results? Really? I'll tell you another little secret.

What you are doing is not working. Let me repeat that. What you are doing is not working. You cannot have the same life as now if you want different results. You cannot be the same person. That's what change is. It's not changing the events of your life that will result in a new life. It's changing you that will result in a new life. It's changing yourself. It's changing myself.

It's changing how you will act, and changing how you act can only occur if you change your thoughts. And if you want to rapidly change you thoughts, and as a result your actions, your life, then how you think must be radically different to how you think now. It may have to be the polar opposite, or at least it will feel like the polar opposite. If you are a reckless person, then what you have to feel and think is more that just moderation. You'll have to feel like you are being totally risk-averse. If you are a smoker, you have to make yourself feel like a non-smoker. If you want to change, you have to change your character. You don't change life, and then you yourself changes or not. You change yourself, and then life changes, or not. You have to change who you have been up until this point. You cannot be the same person. You cannot. Please dwell on it.

Do you really want to become a different person? Are you sure? If you are sure, then I think I can help you.

Key Points

1. You have to really want to change.
2. We can create the emotional intensity to change.
3. Only two things can be guaranteed when it comes to change.
4. You may feel like you are going in the wrong direction.
5. You don't know the full extent of your capabilities.
6. You have to believe the evidence of your own senses.
7. You cannot ignore the results of your actions.
8. You have to change yourself if you want a new life.
9. You have to think in a radically different way.

Exercises

1. What do you want to change in life?

Write down everything you can think of that you want to change. Change your life. Change your job. Change your body. Change your thoughts. Anything you can think of.

2. What do you think your current capabilities are?

Write down everything you can think of that you could do in the past. Write down everything that you think you can do now. Write down everything you think you will be able to do in the future.

3. Repeat the following phrase for a minimum of five minutes, and try to do it with as much intensity as you like. You may do it out loud if you want. If you don't want to be heard, just say it to yourself in you mind.

"I really want to change."

You can change if you really want to.

CHAPTER 3. THREE NECESSARY BELIEFS

What is motivation? I think we can agree that it's the ability to get ourselves to do things. I'm motivated to write this to help you. You're motivated to read this to help yourself. By the way, I can't help you directly. I can help you help yourself. It will only come from within yourself. It's a bit corny, but the power to change is within you. It's not in anything outside you. You can only learn techniques from others.

But learning them doesn't really matter. You have the power to discover the techniques yourself. It may take a lot longer to figure them out, but of course you can. There's nothing about anyone that is better than you. We all have different experiences, and that why we learn. Why just learn from your own experiences when you can learn from others too? I've never understood people who weren't interested in the experiences of others. I'm guessing your not one of those people.

But maybe you are. That's not in itself fundamentally bad, but I do have something that I would like you to do before you continue reading. Could you please rediscover electricity? Stop what you are doing, and think about how to find electricity. How would you do it? I'm not saying walk to an electricity socket and point. What I'm saying is, what things would

35

you have to believe before you could rediscover electricity without referring to anything that you have learned before? I'm not saying it's impossible, but it would take a very long time.

So instead of trying to rediscover electricity, I will give you my discovery, my technique. Of course it builds on other techniques, but I believe it's a bit more effective. We are all just building on the experiences of others that came before us. That's how society has progressed. So what we have to do is educate ourselves, either from others, or from ourselves, about our ability to get ourselves to act.

This ability is within ourselves. We get up in the morning. We brush our teeth. We wash. We eat. We go to work. We work. We come home. We rest. We sleep. No-one is forcing us to do these things. We choose to do them. You may feel like you have no choice but to do these things. That's perfectly natural. No one wants a bank breathing down their neck for mortgage payments. No-one wants their landlord complaining about late rent, or worse. No-one wants to sleep on the street. We believe we are capable of acting. You have to believe that you can do things. It's pretty obvious.

So that's what I'll call belief number 1: We are capable of acting.

But do you really believe you can do anything? Do you believe that you can run a marathon? Unless you have some physical limitation, which you probably didn't choose, I believe you can.

"I'm too old"

I've seen some people in their 70's run marathons.

"I'm too heavy"

Well, you may be at the beginning of your marathon training, but I'm sure you won't be at the end of it. I've seen all people of different shapes and sizes run marathons. It may not seem probable at the moment, but it's not impossible for the majority of people. What about something a bit easier?

What about writing a novel? If you are able to create a sentence, and you are able to describe something, then I have no doubt that you can. That's just what a novel is. A series of descriptive sentences.

"Well, I don't know what to write!"

You have a story already within you. Your life. You may even think you have the most boring life of anyone you ever met. You could even write about how boring you are! But I don't believe that's true.

There's something interesting about everyone. And there is something unique within everyone that you won't find somewhere else. An experience or skill that someone else could learn from. It may be similar to another persons, but it would be uniquely theirs. There is always an opportunity to learn from someone else.

So belief number 2 is: You have to believe you are capable of doing a specific thing.

Or perhaps, you should think of it a different way. You have to believe you are not capable of not doing a specific thing. If I asked you to stop brushing you teeth today, and for the next 100 days. What would you say? How would you feel? You may give it a try, but after a day or two you'd brush your teeth. Why is that? What if you could feel the same way about anything you wanted to do? What if you could make yourself unable to not act towards your goal? Is it impossible? No. Is it improbable? No. You already do it a lot of the time. You can't stop yourself from doing many things. You can't stop yourself from eating. You can't stop yourself from washing. You can't stop yourself from working. You can't stop yourself from being a loving person.

"But I already know how to do those things. What about things I don't know how to do?"

That's the key result of this method that I will teach you later. You'll not be able to not act towards what you want if you continually use this technique.

And that's belief number 3: You can't not do nothing towards your goal.

This may seem improbable at the moment if you haven't been able to do anything towards your goal. But I reckon you could do something towards your goal which you may not have already done. You can write it down. Yes that's all. And just look at it. Every day. Repeat the words in your head.

"So how is looking at my written goal supposed to help me? It's just a piece of paper"

After a few days you'll begin to feel the desire to do something. You'll feel a little uncomfortable. Maybe you'll feel it in the pit of your stomach. Maybe you'll feel ashamed that you have not completed this goal yet. That's good. If you feel nothing, then you won't be able to move towards your goal. You won't be determined enough without any emotion.

You may even feel terrible when you look at your goal. Why Is that? Because you are aware of what you really want, and you are not doing anything towards it. You have to know what you want before you can move towards it, and you have to feel it. If it's just some vague thought in your head, you won't do anything towards it.

If you write it down you begin to realize that you might be nowhere near completing it, or that it would in fact take less effort than you originally thought. So maybe you need even more emotions about your goal?

Key Points

1. You can only learn techniques from others.
2. Why just learn from your own experiences when you can learn from others too?
3. We are all just building on the experiences of others that came before us.
4. We have to believe we are capable of acting.
5. You have to believe you are capable of doing a specific thing.
6. You can't stop yourself from doing many things.
7. You can't not do nothing towards your goal.
8. You have to know what you want before you can move towards it, and you have to feel it.

Exercises

1. Write down a list of things that you cannot not do at the moment.

Look at different areas of your life and think about what you cannot not do. For example, you cannot not brush your teeth. You cannot not take out the rubbish. You cannot not be vegetarian, if that is your belief. You cannot not speak politely.

2. Write down a list of things that you wish you could do, but can't do at the moment.

Again look at different areas of your life. Write down any thing you dreamt of doing or being but have not done yet. For example, write a novel. Start your own business. Visit a natural wonder of the world.

3. Repeat for a minimum of five minutes the following phrase for the three most important things on your list:

"I am worthy enough to <insert the thing you dreamt of doing or being>"

"I am worthy enough to write a novel."

"I am worthy enough to start my own business."

"I am worthy enough to visit the Grand Canyon."

CHAPTER 4. UNACCEPTABLE

If you are not too bothered about reaching a goal, no amount of help, or money, will help you move yourself towards it. If it really was such an important goal to you, you would hate every second when you were not moving towards it.

"But I just don't feel that much about it. I kind of want it."

Just kind of wanting a goal will not lead you anywhere. You kind of wanting to lose weight will just not motivate you. You kind of wanting to be a good father or mother will also not motivate you. You have to want it so much that you feel sick of thought of you not getting it. You have to feel so much emotion in yourself that you can't stop yourself. Not achieving your goal has to become unacceptable to you.

What would be unacceptable to you? It differs for different people. Some people would be not too bothered by saying something that made themselves look stupid. Other people may feel dread at the thought of being thought to be stupid, and as a result they may hesitate in saying anything at all. For some people, not losing 10 pounds in weight after stating to all that they are on diet would be humiliating. For others, they would just shrug it off if they hadn't lost the weight they expected to. Who do you think is more likely to reach their weight loss goal? I think it's obvious.

People don't do radical things to situations they don't really care about. Do you think that people who perform at the highest levels of sport don't care about what they do? Of course they do. They love it. The ups and downs. The heartache of losing spurs some sportspeople to improve themselves. The heartache also makes some sportspeople want to throw in the towel and just give up. Well you can give up a sport and do something else. You can change your career, and do something else. You can't give up on life. Well, you can, but it's never better than living.

And if you don't really care about it, and yet nevertheless you want it, then you'll have to change how you feel about it. How do you change the way you feel about it? Do you jump and down shouting at the top of your voice? You could try! But I don't feel that's really necessary. You need to change your thoughts until you feel unstoppable.

Some people may want you to go calmly and steadily towards your goal. Just quietly accept your life, move slowly and surely to where you want to get. You can do this, but it's so slow. And haven't we wasted enough time already? We need change to happen rapidly. We need to lift ourselves to the next level. Have you ever noticed that people who tell you to be cautious are usually not successful themselves?

Ideally, you should be cautious and calm, but if it doesn't make you change quickly then it's not effective. You must have emotion backing you up and pushing you forwards. You need that feeling of when a situation is no longer acceptable. You know the feeling. You may have had someone treat you badly and you think to yourself: no more! And then you change the situation.

And if you have the emotion it won't even feel like you are being pushed forward. Obstacles that were in your way in the past will simply dissolve. They can't compete with your new found passion. It will feel effortless. When you get in the correct emotional frame of mind nothing can stop you.

But just pumping yourself up is not enough. Jumping up and down. Waving your arms in the air. High-fiving. It's all meaningless if you don't really believe that you can attain your goal. It's just play acting, and even though it does affect the way you feel. It's not enough. It's not enough to get you to do whatever it takes to succeed at your goal.

To succeed at anything, you have to feel it in every part of you. You have to think its simply inevitable that you will succeed. And if anyone or anything gets in your way, you will simply go around them. If anyone tries to hold you back, you will simply ignore them.

And that person may exist at the back of your mind. If you have enough emotion, you won't take no from yourself. You'll act. The negativity never goes away, but you will ignore it. Neither positivity or negativity will be what is driving you. Inevitability will be the driving force. It's your turn to succeed. It's not optional. There is no question of whether it's a matter of choice. It's your time.

It's your time to move towards your goal. You will be fearful, and apprehensive, but you know that there's no choice. We don't have a choice as to whether we succeed or not. The thought of not achieving our goals is unacceptable. We will not be stopped. It's unacceptable that you do not have the life of your dreams. It's unacceptable for all of us. We must create that feeling within us. We have to have the life we want. And we are going to do it together.

Key Points

1. Just kind of wanting a goal will not lead you anywhere.
2. Not achieving your goal has to become unacceptable to you.
3. People don't do radical things to situations they don't really care about.
4. You need that feeling of when a situation is no longer acceptable.
5. When you get in the correct emotional frame of mind nothing can stop you.
6. You have to think its simply inevitable that you will succeed.
7. If you have enough emotion, you won't take no from yourself.
8. We don't have a choice as to whether we succeed or not.

Exercises

1. Do you remember a time when something in you life was acceptable but is now unacceptable?

Write down anything that is unacceptable to you. Write down anything that was acceptable to you in the past and now is unacceptable. You may have cursed and sworn in the past but now it's unacceptable to you. You may have smoked in the past but now you don't and it's unacceptable to you.

2. Do you have any regrets?

Write down any regrets you have. Write down in as much detail why you regret each one. What would you do different if you had the chance? What would your advice be to someone who was in a similar situation?

3. Repeat for at least five minutes the following phrase for the top three things that are unacceptable in your life.

"It is unacceptable that <insert unacceptable thing>"
"It is unacceptable that I do not have enough money."

"It is unacceptable that I do not have love in my life."

"It is unacceptable that I am unhealthy."

You have to believe that you are in
an unacceptable situation if you want to change.

CHAPTER 5. THE TEMPLATE

So if your goals were inevitable, what would you choose? If you knew that you would eventually accomplish any goal you chose, what would you choose?

Lose weight. Be a parent. Own a home. Be a really good friend. Having your own business. Having a significant other. Being the best lover for your significant other. Being happy every day. Being the best sportsperson. Stopping smoking. Stopping negativity. Changing every part of your life. Being the richest person alive!

Are any of these things impossible? Of course not. Has someone on this planet done it before? Of course. So what's the problem? Why don't you have what you want yet? Because you don't know what you want.

"What? I just told you what I want."

No. It's just what you kind of want. If your goal is to lose weight, did you just say my goal is to lose weight. A good goal. One that many, including myself, have achieved, or have to achieve. But to state a goal like that doesn't really say anything.

I want to fly to the moon. Ok… So how would I do it? Flap my arms and fly? Of course not. I would have to create all the things before that were necessary to be able to fly to the moon. That seems obvious. So, say for example, you want to lose weight, do you have all the things you need to lose weight at your disposal?

Do you have a pair of walking shoes, or gym shoes? Because you are going to have to move your body daily. Do you have a fridge filled with healthy ingredients? Because you won't be able to get a lighter body by eating unhealthy foods. Do you have a good healthy eating recipe book? Because you need to create meals that you will enjoy whilst you body returns to a lighter weight.

But it's not enough to just have these things to lose weight. If you want to buy healthy foods, you have to know what are healthy foods, and you need a shopping list. To say simply that you need to lose weight is not enough, you need to find as many resources as possible to help you lose weight. If you want to start your own business you need to find as many resources to help you start your own business. Otherwise you're just improvising and you could spend a whole life just improvising and hoping for the best.

So if you ever want to achieve a goal it's necessary for you to understand what it takes to achieve that goal. And to understand what it takes to achieve a goal quickly with the least amount of mistakes, you must educate yourself. Why just learn from your own experiences?

If someone has done something before, learn from them. It is a template for you to follow. Copy them. Build upon what they have taught you. Why waste time? No more wasted time! Wasting time to get to your goals should become unacceptable to you. Buy the best books. Find the best teachers. What are you waiting for? Why are you listening to this? Get on with it. Wait. At least finish the book.

If you can read this, then you can acquire the knowledge you need to reach your goals, but even then it's not enough to just know what to do. You may already know everything that you need to do, but you still don't do anything towards your goal. Why is that?

If you know what to do and you want to do it, what's stopping you? Do you need more knowledge? No. Do you need more desire? No. Something is holding you back. Maybe you believe you are not worthy of the goal. For some reason, you believe that you don't deserve the goal. That you are not good enough. That whenever you try something, you eventually fail, and therefore you are a loser.

Has anyone ever actually said that to you? "Why are you doing that, you're going to fail!" It's certainly possible that you have had or have a person like that in your life. Just tell them you choose to try, and if you fail, you fail.

My advice would be to run a mile from anyone who says you shouldn't try something towards your goal that you know has worked for someone else. You really don't have time to waste with people like that. It's not about being positive or negative with you. It's about being supportive of you when you are trying your hardest. If someone doesn't want to support you when you are heading towards your goal, then they don't deserve to come with you as you head towards your goal.

Life really is too short. It's hard especially when it's someone who you really care about, or someone who you really don't want to part with. A possible solution is to ask them what they think you should do. If they say your goal is impossible, you know they are wrong. And the only thing that will convince them is results.

I can understand not having the confidence in something until it delivers, but you have to have a period before you have any results. You have to have a period where nothing is happening. Like a seed under the soil, until it sprouts, you must be open-minded to see if it will sprout.

Some people call it faith that it will happen. I think that's too strong. Open minded to the possibility of a good result is a better way to look at it. Do you want to stop going for the goal because you didn't see any instant results? If all you needed was just a little patience, then wouldn't it be worth it? If you had to wait just one week for the proof that you were heading towards your goal, wouldn't you wait? You'd be silly not to.

Key Points

1. If you knew that you would eventually accomplish any goal you chose, what would you choose?
2. You don't know what you want.
3. You have to have all the things that are necessary to be successful at a goal before you can succeed at a goal.
4. If someone has done something before, learn from them. It is a template for you to follow.
5. You can acquire the knowledge you need to reach your goals.
6. You may believe you are not worthy of the goal.
7. People that don't support you when you are heading towards your goal, don't deserve to come with you as you head towards your goal.
8. If someone says your goal is impossible, the only thing that will convince them is results.
9. You have to have a period where nothing is happening like a seed waiting to sprout.

Exercises

1. Have you ever done something that you knew you wouldn't fail at?

Write down anything that you knew you wouldn't fail at. And then list everything you would do if you knew you could not fail. For example: Start a business. Own a home. Be a father. Lose weight. Be the best friend anyone would want.

2. What is the most important goal that you want to accomplish?

Write down your most important goal. List all the things that you can think of at the top of your head that you will need. Don't worry if you can't think of much. If we don't know what to do, then we must find out from someone else what to do.

3. Repeat for at least five minutes the following phrase:

"I can do anything that someone else has done."

Repeat this enough times and you will begin to see everywhere around you, the new truth that you know about yourself, that you can do exactly the same thing as someone else.

You can do anything that someone else has done.

CHAPTER 6. THERE ARE NO DIFFICULT GOALS

Have you ever mowed a lawn? Or have you ever caught a bus? Have you ever just missed a bus? Did you pass at least one exam at school? Can you cook a meal? Have you passed a driving test? Have you done anything in life that you wanted to do? Of course you have. If you're like me, then you also haven't done a lot of things that you wanted to do too. But you have lived and you've succeeded and you've failed

So why do you believe that you can't have the life of your dreams?

"Well it's just been too difficult up to now."

It may well have been too difficult up to now. And that's the key phrase: "up to now". If you believe that something is too difficult you'll find the way to make it feel difficult. You'll be negative. You'll procrastinate. You'll be nervous. You'll hesitate when you get started. There'll always be something you expect that will make the task hard.

But what about the opposite? What if you believed the task was easy? Would you get nervous?

Would you procrastinate? Would you be negative? No. Of course not. You'd just do it.

Now I'm not saying anything about the actual task here. Of course some tasks are harder than others. Building a house is much more difficult than building a shed. Building a cruise ship is more difficult than building a row boat. But if you believe that building a row boat was extraordinarily difficult, you'd never get started. And if you believed that building your own cruise ship was extraordinarily easy, and it was something you really wanted, you'd at least find some way to move towards it. Even if at that moment it seems like a crazy goal.

In some ways you are building your own cruise ship to take you anywhere you have wanted to go. You are creating a vehicle to take you to where you want to go. That vehicle is yourself. If you believe that changing yourself to create a better life is difficult, then it's going to seem more difficult to you. If you believe that changing your life is quite easy, then it's going to seem easy to you.

Of course there are many details to be looked at and tasks that must be completed. However chaining yourself down before you have even stood up will make your task much harder. You have to believe that accomplishing the goal is easy but that it requires a lot of tasks to get there and that it's necessary to complete some tasks before you can complete others.

If you really wanted to build a cruise ship then you would have to do a lot of things just to get to the point of constructing it. You'd have to design it, you'd have to find a way to fund it's construction. You'd have to find a place to build it. You have to gather a team to build it. Another team to test it. And another team to run it.

A lot of people conflate the difficulty of a goal with the time it would take to reach the goal. And it really is a fallacy to even suggest that goals are something that can be easy or difficult. There are simply goals that take more time and have more steps than other goals. There are more steps and tasks required to build a cruise ship. Thousands more. But each task is in itself not difficult. It just is. It's either done or not done.

You may need to educate yourself before you can perform a task. But there is no inherent difficulty in the task. It's us who ascribe a level of ease or difficulty to a task based on what prior tasks must be completed before we can do it. But each of those prior tasks are not inherently difficult themselves. There are just lots of them so it's natural that it would take more time to get to your goal.

So to say you can't do something that appears difficult to you, is in reality, to say that it would take a lot of small tasks prior to completing the goal that you haven't yet performed. That's all. It took thousands upon thousands of small tasks from the time when you were born until this moment now to make you into the person you are now. There will be thousands upon thousands more tasks in the future to come. And you are capable of performing every single one.

The problem is that you're believing the voice in your head. But that's all it is. It's a voice. It's not reality. It's just an interpretation of reality, and it's your choice to decide whether it does in fact reflect reality or it's just an incorrect interpretation.

Goals simply either take more or less time and have more or less steps. It's your choice as to whether you want to commit yourself to completing all the steps to get to the goal. But of course you can do it. Nothing and nobody is stopping you but your commitment to focus on a particular goal.

The only person who is stopping you is yourself, and that's because of some unfortunate and incorrect beliefs that you have been led to believe are true. It's not your fault what people taught you as child. But now you choose your own life, and thoughts, you can choose to be whoever you want to be, and I know one hundred percent that if you commit to the goal, and you learn or discover all the steps and tasks, that you will achieve your goal. I know that you are unstoppable. I know because I am too.

Key Points

1. You have lived and you've succeeded and you've failed.
2. You have to give up your belief that a goal is difficult.
3. You will hesitate to act towards a goal if you believe it is difficult.
4. If you believe that changing your life is quite easy, then it's going to seem easy to you.
5. There are simply goals that take more time and have more steps than other goals.
6. We ascribe a level of ease or difficulty to a task based on what prior tasks must be completed before we can do it.
7. Your inner voice is just an interpretation of reality.
8. Nothing and nobody is stopping you but your commitment to focus on a particular goal.

Exercises

1. Is there something that you want to do that seems very difficult to you?

Write down anything you want to do that seems very difficult to you. Absolutely anything. Do you want to learn how to paint? Do you want to create a beautiful garden? Do you want to climb the highest mountain on your continent?

2. Is there something that you do now that seems very easy to you?

Write down anything that you do now that seems very easy to you. It could be something like driving a car, or playing a sport, or dealing with difficult people. Any skill that you do effortlessly. Then write down all the steps it took for you to get there.

3. Repeat the following phrase for at least five minutes:

"I can complete each task"

Any time you have a lot of tasks that you want to do, just repeat this phrase and you will believe that you can do them. Of course some tasks will not be completed fully at one particular time, but part of it can be, and at another time, you will be able to complete another part.

You can complete any task you set your mind to.

CHAPTER 7. OPTIMISTIC VIGILANCE

Have you ever succeeded at something, and you were really positive and it turned out roughly how you expected it to? Of course you have, I hope. You expected to succeed and you did. Alternatively, have you ever succeeded at something, you were really negative about, and it didn't turn out as you expected? You expected to fail, but you didn't, you succeeded. I know this feeling very well.

So I think we can agree that you may succeed at something whilst being positive or negative. Have you ever felt nothing about a goal, yet nevertheless you succeeded? You were just open-minded to whatever possibility occurred. Whereas when we are positive or negative about succeeding at something, we are being narrow-minded about the possible outcome. We have closed off in our mind the possibility that there are different possibilities.

Either being positive or negative is not the absolute best way to feel when pursuing a goal. However, they are useful tools. Being positive is a great way to get yourself moving towards a goal you want to happen. Sometimes you may hesitate to act if you believed it would fail from the very beginning. You wouldn't even attempt to train for a marathon if you were certain you would fail.

Likewise, being negative is a great way to think if it motivates you to prevent something very bad from happening. You put on a seat belt because you think of the possibility of something very bad happening if you did not. Even though it's extremely unusual to have an accident, you don't fail to put your seat belt on because you are positive that nothing bad will happen.

However you shouldn't fret and worry that something bad will happen. You may never get into the car! Nevertheless, you shouldn't happily ignore that something bad might not happen. You may let your guard down and then something really bad will happen. So neither positivity or negativity is ideal.

You need to be open to the possibility that either situation might occur. You need to be vigilant and optimistic too. It's what I call, using all the powers of my creativity: optimistic vigilance. Thinking of all of the bad things that might happen, guarding against them, and then still acting. You can't be paralyzed by fear, but you can't be carried away with hubris.

You have to act. You have no choice. You won't succeed at anything if you don't do something. But you won't succeed if you just do anything because you were "just being positive". You can't be overcautious, but you can't not be cautious. You have to act, but just don't be stupid about it.

You have to do things you would never do before. It's the only way to progress. It bears repeating that you won't get different results by doing the same thing again and again. Whenever you want something in your life to change, you have to change what you do. And often what you have to do may feel a little discomforting, and that should happen when you are thinking and acting in a different way. You're breaking out of your every day pattern.

For example, can you swim? Can you cycle? I've been able to cycle since I was eight years old. I love it, I didn't for many years, but I never forgot, and I wasn't fearful when I began again. On the other hand, I never learnt to swim as a child, or as a teenager, or as a young adult, or as slightly older adult. I learnt to swim at 43!

I feel like I am still a beginner, but I can swim...on my front. Was I fearful when I first went into the pool to learn? A little. I had never floated before in my life. Was I going to give up? Of course not. If someone else can swim I can too. It was just a matter of technique. I was floating in less that twenty minutes, and swimming by the end of the 30 minute class. By the end of the week of classes I was loving it. The next challenge is to learn to swim on my back. I broke through my comfort zone before, and I need to break through my comfort zone again, and again, and again.

To progress at a task, or absolutely anything, you have to be continually breaking through your comfort zones. Once you get comfortable, you need to get uncomfortable quick if you want to improve at anything. An easy way to do this is to always focus on something that you have very little experience in, or the least amount of experience in doing, or on something that up to now you have had very little success at.

If you have always been a bit shy with people and you think that's something you are not very good at, then you must do something which you would associate a non-shy person doing. It may be failing to greet someone. So the solution is to always be the first to greet someone when you see them. After 10 times, you'll wonder why you ever thought it was difficult to do. Trust me. This was once me.

We have to continually do the things we have never done before. We must not believe there is some limit within us that is stopping us. There are of course people who will try to limit our successes, but there is not a limit to what we can do. There are no limits. None. We can be anything. So what's stopping you?

Key Points

1. You may succeed at something whilst being positive or negative.
2. Being positive or negative closes off in our minds the possibility that there are different possibilities.
3. Being positive is a great way to get yourself moving towards a goal you want to happen.
4. Being negative is a great way to think if it motivates you to prevent something very bad from happening.
5. You need to be vigilant and optimistic too.
6. You won't get different results by doing the same thing again and again.
7. You have to be continually breaking through your comfort zones.
8. There is no limit within us that is stopping us.

Exercises

1. Have you ever been positive or negative about something and what really happened didn't match your expectations?

Write down an experience like this. If you are like me, you may have many experiences. Write them down. Can you see that neither way of thinking was correct?

2. Have you ever done something that took you out of your comfort zone?

Write it down. See? You've done it before you can do it again and again and again. If the task seems too large to handle, break it down to the smallest possible step. If you were planning a wedding and you were paralyzed by all things you needed to do and you could never get started, then you could choose the simplest thing you could possibly do. Pick up a pen and a piece of paper. Or turn on your computer and open a word processing document. That's all. Now think of the next simplest step and so on.

3. Repeat the following phrase for at least five minutes:

"There are no limits to what I can do."

There aren't any limits to what you can do. And it's not being positive or optimistic. It's the truth whether you like it or not.

74

CHAPTER 8. THE BEGINNING OF THE END

Do you understand why you need to stop procrastinating? Of course! To get things done fast! What a silly question! Well, on the surface it is, however it's not working is it? We know that we want to get things done quickly, efficiently, and effectively. But if we know that, why is it not happening? Why aren't we doing things quickly? What's stopping us sometimes?

I have another question, perhaps a little personal, I apologize in advance. Do you procrastinate when you really need to go to the bathroom? Of course you don't! Well, I hope you don't. You just do it, you just go, no-one and nothing is going to stop you. The consequences of not going, as you know, would be too horrible to bear. And if you ever know anyone who eventually becomes unable to control themselves, have some sympathy and understanding, it's something you wouldn't want to wish on anyone you care dearly for.

The clue is in why you act without hesitation. The consequences of not doing it is so bad that you do it without thought. The problem is that you are not conscious, at the time of acting, of the reasons that would motivate you to act. With a strong enough reason, you can do anything instantly. Let me repeat that. With a strong enough reason you can do anything instantly.

Getting things done fast, for you, is not a strong enough reason. Getting things done fast because it will make you more efficient, or because it will help your business grow, or it will make you become a millionaire, or whatever, for you, are not strong enough reasons. Do you want to know why they are not strong enough reasons? Not succeeding at the task wouldn't really affect you that much. Well that's how it appears.

"I'll just go slowly, nothing major will happen!",

"I don't need extra money, you won't take it with you when you die!".

And you would be correct. The reasons for not doing something are often good enough to stop you from doing something.

But that is only because you are not conscious of the consequences of not acting. When you are driving to the airport, do you say to yourself: "I'll just go at my own pace, nothing serious will happen if I miss the plane". Of course, nothing will. Nothing major will happen if you miss your plane. You'll live.

"But if I don't catch it I'll miss my business meeting! I'll lose my job. That's major!"

No. You'll find another job. You'll live.

"But I spent thousands on this holiday! It's my dream!". You'll lose some money. You'll live. Well, what is a strong enough reason? Act as if your life depended on it? It's not really motivating. It's not something you can imagine. And anyway, I've had a good life. I'm happy, I'm content...

So, what is a strong enough reason? The reason you believe to be good enough. That's it. For one person, the humiliation of losing their job because they missed their plane is a good enough reason. For another person, me for example, losing the money I spent on a cheap flight to a cheap hotel is enough to motivate me to get us to the airport early. The actual reason doesn't matter. It's what the reason means to you that matters.

So if you want to act instantly, you must create the reason that would motivate you, and that reason needs to be within the very fiber of your being. Once that reason gets into you, nothing will stop you, ever. Nothing will stop you from acting, in fact you'll feel uneasy and restless at the thought of not doing it. You will become the opposite of what you were. A person who couldn't do a particular thing who now couldn't not do that particular thing.

I think you understand, but I'll give you an example from my life. I never use to shave everyday. I use to trim my fashionable beard once a week. I hated shaving. I hated trimming my beard too, but I did it because I didn't want to look too messy. Now, I shave every day without hesitation. I can't not shave. So was it some kind of magical spell that made me become the opposite? No of course not! Was it self-discipline? No. Will-power? No.

I simply have a reason that is strong enough to motivate me to act everyday without fail and that reason is hard-wired within me. My reason is that my wife likes a smooth face when I kiss her, or when she kisses me. It's not a magical reason, it's not some all powerful reason.

"Act as if your life depended on it!"

Really? For shaving? It doesn't seem true and it's not. Be truthful. You're not going to motivate yourself with what you believe to be a lie or by lying to yourself. If you really don't want to help people in poverty, then trying to use it as a reason to get wealthy, and then becoming a philanthropist, will not work. It won't motivate you to act. You may have other reasons that could motivate you to become wealthy, but if you don't really believe in a specific reason, then you're not going to be motivated by that specific reason.

But what if I don't know how to create a strong enough reason to act? We'll come to that later. I know the feeling. Wanting to change, but not seeming to have the power to do so. So many wasted years. I don't want any more wasted years in my life. I don't want you to have any wasted years. No more wasted years. For me, for you, for your loved ones, for my loved ones.

I have a strong enough reason to write this, by helping you do what I now can do, maybe you will help me, and you have by buying this short, but I hope, powerful book. So I have to deliver. You put your faith in me, and I have to do whatever I can to show you that your judgment was correct.

Key Points

1. With a strong enough reason, you can do anything instantly.
2. It often appears that not succeeding at the task wouldn't really affect you that much.
3. What the reason means to you is what matters.
4. You will feel uneasy and restless at the thought of not acting.
5. You're not going to motivate yourself by lying to yourself.

Exercises

1. What things can you do without hesitation?

Write them down. Perhaps a friend calls you and they need your help, you help unquestioningly. You remember that you need to do the dishes before you go out, and you do them without a seconds thought.

2. What are the most important things in your life?

Write them down. It could be anything. It could be your health. Your wealth. Your family. Your home. Your comic book collection. You'd be surprised at what some people consider important. Everyone is different, but what is important to you is a fundamental part of what motivates you.

3. Repeat the following phrase for at least five minutes:

"With a strong enough reason, I can do anything."

There must be examples in your life where your strong reasons have made you change your life in some way. The fact you have changed at all is a sign that you had a strong reason for each example of change.

With a strong enough reason, you can do anything.

CHAPTER 9. THE DISCIPLINED SELF

I'm going to tell you a secret which may seem unusual to read: I have no self-discipline. Zero. Nothing.

"Surely, you have the self-discipline to write? That's what you're doing!"

Yes, that's correct, I am writing. Does it require any self-discipline to write it? Am I straining and struggling to control myself whilst I type these words? Am I trying to stop myself from drinking this cup of coffee next to me? No. I'm just typing. It's effortless. There's no self-discipline involved.

"Well, you must have the self-discipline to plan, think, research, and sit and write each day until you've completed. The words are not just flowing out of you like some kind of magical fountain of knowledge!".

No, there's no self-discipline involved. I'm not trying, I'm just doing.

Maybe, we disagree on what "self-discipline" is? What is it that most people consider to be self-discipline? I think a good definition is:

The ability to do what you want when you want.

Here are some examples involving what many consider to be self-discipline, which I think we can reasonably agree on: I can write/read this sentence without being distracted. I can run for 20 minutes. I can eat healthily all day. I take the dog for a walk every evening without fail. I can study for 1 hour. I can wake up at 5 am and write. I can be romantic to my wife by never forgetting to buy flowers.

There are also many examples of what people in general consider to be a lack of self-discipline. I said I would eat healthily today, but I can't resist this piece of cake. I said I would no longer smoke, but I'll just have one more. I thought I was going to exercise today, but I think I'll just relax by watching a film.

When we are said to have self-discipline, we do or not do something that matches our desire of what we want to do or not do. And when we are said to lack self-discipline, we do or not do something that doesn't match our desire of what we want to do or not do. Really? Is this true?

When you ate that piece of chocolate cake instead of an apple, is it something you didn't want to do? No, of course not. Your desire to eat the piece of chocolate cake was stronger than your desire to eat an apple. You did something that matched your desire of what you wanted to do. You simply had competing things that you wanted to do that could not be done at exactly the same time.

See here's the key to what many people think about self-discipline. You either have self-discipline, or you have a lack of self-discipline. It's considered to be a quality that exists in ourselves in relation to a particular action or circumstance. But there is a problem with this way of thinking.

How can a person have self-discipline in one area of their life, but not have self-discipline in another area? I mean, you already know how to have self-discipline with, for example, alcohol. You don't drink a whole bottle of rum if it's placed in front of you, but you can't resist a piece of delicious chocolate cake, even though you said you would no longer eat delicious, yummy, the kind you can't just get enough of, chocolate cake.

Surely, if you know how to have self-discipline in one area, you should instantly know how to have self-discipline in another. But you don't apply what you know. Why is it that you can't instantly turn on your self-discipline? Life would be much easier. We'd choose a goal, be self-disciplined, and then achieve our goal. Well, you don't apply what you know, because….there is nothing to know. It doesn't exist.

What you consider to be self-discipline is in fact something else that has nothing to do with your capacity to act or not.

You are always doing what you want to do when you want. You never do what you don't want to do. When you were still doing something that you said you no longer wanted to do, you were still doing what you wanted to do. When you eventually stop doing something you no longer want to do, you are doing what you want to do.

There is no capacity in yourself called self-discipline and once you fully understand that you are able to begin to do whatever you want when you want, which is what many consider to be the quality of self-discipline.

There are simply competing desires that you want to have fulfilled at the same time and one of those desires has reasons for it that are stronger for you at that particular time. And those reasons make it what you want to do at that time.

If you want to do something different to what you normally do, then you need to get stronger reasons for it than the reasons for what you normally do.

'Wait a minute, that sounds a bit wacky, of course there is self-discipline. How on earth do I get anything done? I don't just do random things. I choose to do this, and I choose to not do that."

Of course that's true. But why do you still choose to do things that deep down you wish you didn't do, but you do nonetheless? You may even be conscious of the consequences of doing it, and they may be extremely negative, and you still do it. You may know that smoking is deadly, and you know all the science behind the claim, but you still do it. Because reasons, even very strong reasons, to do or not do something are not enough.

Reasons are a necessary component, but by themselves they are not sufficient enough to get you to act without hesitation every time in a particular situation. That's why sometimes you can resist that delicious chocolate cake and other times you can't. You need to hard-wire your self. And it's possible to do it so that you never eat another piece again, but why would you want to do that. After all, it's delicious. But you can, if you so choose.

You always knew right? There is nothing wrong with you. You've been taught to believe that you were deficient in some way, me too, I always believed I was lacking in some way, I just didn't have the right stuff, the true grit, the self-discipline to get things done. Well, you can't be lacking in a quality that doesn't exist! Did you sigh in relief?

Maybe you're still skeptical, which is perfectly normal. Take a sip of water, take a deep breath, everything you want is within your grasp. We're going to do it together. Me and you. There are no limits to what you and I can do. If they do not break some fundamental scientific law of nature, we can do it, and if we choose to, we will.

Key Points

1. Self-discipline is the ability to do what you want when you want.
2. When we have self-discipline, we do or not do something that matches our desire of what we want to do or not do.
3. Often you simply have competing desires that can not be done at exactly the same time.
4. Why is it that we can't instantly turn on our self-discipline? It doesn't exist.
5. One out of number of competing desires has reasons for it that are stronger than others at that particular time.
6. Reasons are not enough to get you to act without hesitation every time in a particular situation.

Exercises

1. What areas of your life do you have, or have not, what most people consider as self-discipline?

Write down any disciplined action you can think of that you do often. For example, brushing your teeth daily is a disciplined action. Getting up, washing, going to work. These are disciplined actions. And write down any undisciplined action that you really wish didn't happen, but you nevertheless still do.

2. Is there ever a time in your life when you did something that appeared to need self-discipline but you did it quite easily.

Write it down. Maybe you wanted to learn how to dance and it came quite naturally to you. Maybe the thought of you getting up and speaking in public scared you, but it was quite easily nevertheless.

3. Repeat the following phrase for at least 5 minutes.

"I do not need self-discipline to get what I want."

Once you realize this, everything begins to get much easier. The belief that you need self-discipline is holding you back.

CHAPTER 10. THE POWER OF THE WILL

So guess what? Not only do I believe I have no thing called self-discipline, but I also believe I have no thing called will-power.

"Well, that's just absurd!"

Is it really? For the same reason that I don't think we have a quality called self-discipline, we don't have a quality called will-power. We simply have different desires that can't be fulfilled at the same time. At that moment, we believe one has stronger, or better reasons, than the other.

Countless times, and I'm sure maybe you've had something similar happen, I've said to myself: "No more cookies, biscuits, and cakes! I'm going to eat healthy now!" But the moment I'm tired, or stressed, or simply too hungry because I haven't eaten anything all day, I'll sneak into the kitchen, and I'll eat three, or four, or maybe five, delicious cookies, or an extra large handful of walnuts, or I'll cut one big slice of cheese, enough for a large sandwich! And I would love it! Of course, that's why we eat these foods, they're delicious. Let's not fool ourselves.

But we know the consequences, we get on the scales in the morning, and nothing has happened. "This diet isn't working!" Well it was until I decided to eat 500 calories just before bed. I bet you know the feeling, or something similar. I'm going to ride my exercise bike for 20 minutes a day, I'm going to walk 30 minutes a day, and in the end we enjoy another episode of a TV show. Well of course we do! It's far more fun to sit and laugh than get on a bike and sweat. The immediate consequences are not serious. Nothing bad will happen to us if eat a cookie, or watch some more TV, at this particular moment. But it all adds up.

I used to smoke. Thankfully, I quit nearly 20 years ago. One of the best things I have ever done. Thankfully, people are smoking less and less. Imagine if I didn't. My lungs would have been filled with 30 years of tar. My skin would have aged. My teeth would be permanently stained. If I didn't have a serious illness, I'm sure I would have had one in the future. I tried to stop more times than I remember.

I just didn't have the will-power. Of course I didn't. It doesn't exist. If you open you mind to the possibility that it doesn't exist, you will begin to see a way to get what you want with almost no effort. Effortless action. Imagine that. Not only is it possible, but it's easier than you think.

I've wasted so many of my years with the false beliefs in my head about will-power and self-discipline. I'm obsessed now. It's my mission. I have to help others break out of this way of thinking. Our lives are being wasted because of these limiting beliefs. We can be so much better than this. If we can give up on the ideas that we need will-power and self-discipline, we can be whatever we want to be.

Why do other people succeed with their goals, but others don't? Do you think they have some kind of magic secret? No. It's not true. They believe they have no limits to what they can do. If you give up on the idea that you need self-discipline and will-power, you will see that there's no limit to what you can do. You only need to act, just do it.

"Well, that's easy to say! How do I just do it? I don't know how to do it."

I understand. I was there too, and there are many things where I don't just act, because I haven't chosen to focus on it yet. But when I choose to, I will succeed, without question. I will explain the method to get anything done later. We are nearly there, we are nearly free to do what we want, when we want, and how we want.

So if what we are doing now requires no will-power, then how is it possible to do anything? A different question would be: why do we keep doing things that we know we don't want to do? At the moment of weakness, or what we believe to be weakness, we still do the thing we promised we would never do again. Why?

It's because at that moment, that's all there is within our minds. At the moment of weakness, our mind needs to tell us to change our behavior. Often it doesn't. It tells us to succumb to our desires. Or worse, we just do things without thought. How many things in our lives do we do without thought? Mindless eating. Mindless internet surfing. Mindless TV watching. Mindless working in a job we hate. But we still do it because we believe we have no choice. Or we believe that we don't know what to do to make ourselves change. Or we believe we don't have the strength to change our lives. You will know soon, and if you follow the method, then not only will you pursue your goals, you will not be able to not pursue your goals.

I hope you choose wisely because once you focus on this method, you will become a different person. I'm not going to tell you what to choose. It's your life. I can tell you what I have chosen, but think about the consequences of the completion of your goals. How would it affect you and the people you care about? But let there be no doubt about it. You have to change. I have to change. We must constantly become different people to reach our goals. And we will be different people when we reach them. Fundamentally, we will be the same, but our belief in ourselves and our capabilities will be very different.

Key Points

1. We love the things that give us pleasure even if they are harmful to us.
2. We don't worry because the immediate consequences are not serious.
3. You have to open your mind to the possibility that will-power doesn't exist.
4. We can be whatever we want to be if we don't need self-discipline and will-power.
5. Why do we keep doing the things that we don't want to do?
6. When we do something that we don't want to do, it's often the only thing in our minds.

Exercises

1. Is there anything you really love to do that you think would need will-power to stop?

Write them down. Eating cake. Smoking. Not exercising. Oh I love cake. There's nothing inherently right or wrong in doing these things. It's your choice to live how you want as long as you are not harming others. However the consequences may be a poorer quality of life due to bad health, or even early, preventable death.

2. If you could stop immediately doing something what would it be?

Write it down. Maybe you really do want to stop but you never believed that it was possible to do because it was so hard. Many people have before therefore so can you, because they are no better than you.

3. Repeat the following phrase for at least 5 minutes:

"I do not need will-power to do anything."

You do have power over your actions but it's not as hard as you have been led to believe.

You do not need will-power to do anything.

CHAPTER 11. THE UNGUIDED BRAIN

I'm going to say something that may be new you to. It may shock you when you think about what it really means. It may seem intuitive. Maybe you already believe it to be true.

You are not your thoughts. The thoughts you have are not you. They are just statements and feelings that appear in your consciousness. Your consciousness is your awareness of yourself and the world around you. I am conscious of my thoughts as I type, the computer, the screen, desk, etc. A lot of the time you can't choose what appears in your consciousness. You feel sick. You feel hungry. You have a memory from your childhood flash before your eyes. At other times, you choose what appears in your consciousness. You think. You daydream. You listen to music. You talk to yourself inside your head, which is perfectly normal. But they are not you.

I think you understand what I mean, but I will give an example. Have you ever had a thought about something that only a few minutes later you realize is not true? Somehow it's appeared in your mind, you think it's right, and then you correct yourself, and you wonder why you thought it. You may even tell someone about your thought, and they correct you in your error.

This is an experience I know all too well. Our minds are giving us an incorrect memory or interpretation of something. We wouldn't knowingly choose to believe something that is wrong and yet our brain tells us something that is not correct. It appeared in our brains but it was wrong.

It's not your fault. It's just your brain giving you some information. As to how it came about is difficult to determine. It's just your brain inventing something out of the vast set of experiences it has stored within it. They are your unintended thoughts.

You are the person who looks at whatever appears in your consciousness. You are the viewer of whatever thoughts pass through your mind. You can choose to interpret what appears in any way you like. You understand what I'm saying. Sometimes a bad thing will happen, and we realize in the future, that it was good for us. It gave us character. Sometimes a good thing happens, and actually over time, it would have been better if it didn't happen. What we experience is not us, but it can change who we become.

Our experiences change us, so in order to change, we must change what we experience, or our interpretation of it. Often we can't change the events that are outside our mind, but we can change our interpretations of them, and we can change our reactions to events. We can change ourselves to relish the things that we once found difficult, and shun the things that were easy. We can make our reactions to the hard things we are confronted with as an excellent opportunity to become stronger, and to become extremely frustrated at a life that isn't going anywhere. We may also do the opposite. We can make ourselves satisfied with whatever life has given us, and we can feel dread whenever a difficult situation or problem occurs. It's our choice.

This offends some people. I can understand why. They have tried to change and simply have been unable to so far. They get stuck in the trap of believing its other people to blame for their woes. Sometimes it is. But we can control our reactions to it. We should use our bad experiences to empower us. We never wish they would have happened. But we will use them to be strong. Stronger than anyone who caused us harm. We will not surrender to them and their malice. We will not be held back by people who caused us harm.

We are going to change ourselves to make ourselves unstoppable. But we need to take back control of our minds. Let me explain. Our brains, our minds, left to its own device will do whatever it wants and interpret whatever it wants however it wants. It's like a car without a driver and a brick on the pedal. It's moving, whether we like it or not, and we have to steer it, whether we like to or not. We can't let any random thought or feeling that comes into our consciousness direct us in life. We can be aware of our sensations and unintended thoughts, but they are not our masters. We have to consciously choose the thoughts in our minds that we want to think of in order to get the results in our life that we want. And this is how we are going to do it.

It has a number of steps that I will go over in more detail in the next three chapters. Firstly we must choose one goal in our life that we want. Yes, just one goal until acting towards is something you can't not do. And then you can choose the next and the next goal. Then we need to sit and analyze the reasons why we must achieve that goal. Thirdly, we need to focus our thoughts on achieving that goal.

We are going to command our minds to take us where we want to go. We are the drivers of the car and we will choose the road we want to go down. The technique is simple and powerful. You may have used something similar before, or still do something similar in respect to some aspects of your life. It's not magic, but once its starts working, you'll understand its power. I wish I knew it years ago.

You just need one method that is quick, effective, and reusable in many different situations. Are you ready to begin? It's time to jump in the rabbit hole.

Key Points

1. You are not your thoughts.
2. False thoughts enter our consciousness.
3. Our minds can give us an incorrect memory or interpretation of something.
4. Your brain invents thoughts out of the vast set of experiences it has stored within it.
5. You are the person who looks at whatever appears in your consciousness.
6. We can change our interpretations and reactions to events.
7. Our brains, our minds, left to its own device will do whatever it wants and interpret whatever it wants however it wants.
8. We are going to command our minds to take us where we want to go.

Exercises

1. Have you ever thought about something that only a few minutes later you realize is not true?

Has this ever happened to you? Write it down. This happens to me quite frequently. I don't think it's unusual for anyone. It's why we have to double-check facts sometimes. Can you see how your mind often gives you false information? It's not your fault. It's just the way it is.

2. Does your mind often wander?

Write down the times of the day when you tend to be distracted. If you are like me, it wanders more that you would like. Distractions are everywhere. So either we eliminate them, or learn to control our reaction to them. The problem with eliminating them is that we will eventually find other things around us to distract us. I think it's better to focus on trying to change our reactions to them.

3. Repeat the following phrase for at least five minutes:

"I will not be distracted by anything. I am totally focused."

When something tries to distract you this phrase will pop up into your head.

You can be totally focused.

CHAPTER 12. THE POWER OF WORDS

Do you believe in magic? You watch a TV show by some magician or other. Waving their hands, they say a few words, and wow, as if by magic, a rabbit comes of a hat. Of course, we don't really believe a rabbit was summoned by the power of their words. But words do have power.

They have the power to inspire us, the power to make us laugh, and the power to make us cry. They can take a control over us so that we can't think of anything else. If you've ever had someone says something nasty to you, you know what it's like. The words stay in your head. You can't get them out until you do something about it. You either forget them, or lift yourself up above them. It could take minutes. It could take years.

There is nothing wrong with words staying in your head if they are the right words. The words that will inspire. The words that will make you appreciate all the beauty in life. The words that will make you get what you want when you want. They do exist. You just need to use them.

"That's so easy to say. Firstly, I don't know what the words are. And secondly, it's hard, I don't have the time"

Do you have thirty minutes a day to devote to a goal? Do you have thirty minutes to make one change that will have a massive impact on your life? If you want, you'll find the way.

You can also use what I will explain here to find more time in your life. Start with five minutes, then ten, and I think after ten you'll find thirty minutes quite easily. You can either do it sitting down, which I find a little more difficult, or do it whilst walking, which is a lot easier for me. But once you follow this process, eventually you will act towards your goal with very little thought, and without the need to go through the process. Then you can begin on your next goal. And if you ever feel like you need to concentrate more on your goal, or you've been slacking, which is perfectly normal, you should begin the process again for a couple of days to wake yourself up.

I would say, from my experience, that it's best to focus on one goal until you act towards it without much effort, and until you react to situations that deviate from your goal with a sense of unease. We want to make it so that heading towards your goal, and living the life that your goal entails, is a part of your everyday natural behavior. How come some people can eat healthily and exercise daily without a lot of effort? And others, find it hard to even walk 20 minutes daily? It's not magic.

Some might say they have made it a habit of exercising and eating healthily. That's true. After a few months of walking every day and eating healthy foods, it's definitely a habit. But what about before it's a habit. How do we even get to the point where we can create a habit effortlessly? You need to change your thoughts before it can become a habit. You need to focus on your thoughts until it's an unconscious habit. A habit where you don't think about whether you should do or not. You just do it. If another person can do it, we can do it too.

So the first thing we need to do is to decide which goal we want to focus on. I'll use one of my goals to give an example. You know the phrase: "The secret of living is giving". At the moment I have a goal of helping as many people as possible get over their inability to move themselves towards their goals. I see it all around me. It drives me nuts. Why should some people be struggling unhappily doing things they don't want to do, whilst others are fulfilled and stress-free? I know how to help people. I have to help people. I want to bring joy into peoples lives. I feel uneasy at the thought of seeing people struggle in the slow lane, whilst others are zooming past.

But I never felt this way before. I couldn't care less. I made myself become this person. I saw a sales training video recently, I can't remember his name, but it changed my outlook towards people completely. He said there are two ways of doing sales. One is to take your product to a customer, try to sell it to them using sales techniques, and if they don't like it, move on to the next person. The newer method is to build friendships with you customers and potential customers. He said if people don't like you, they won't buy from you even if you have the best product in the world.

So I thought to myself, that's where I'm going wrong in life, I need to be friends with as many people as possible, and maybe my family's life will change for the better. So I thought to myself: How do I build friendships? And then the answer came to me in a flash. Help them. Help people. Help every person you come in contact with. If you do whatever it takes to help a person, you will become unforgettable to them. You will have a new friend, and then perhaps they would help you. They wouldn't have to, and it wouldn't affect your friendship. I thought: "Wow!" That's it.

So my goal is: Help people so that I may build friendships, and by building friendships, maybe they will help us. But how do I do this? I then remembered something the great Tony Robbins said: "We all get our musts, we don't get our shoulds." And that became the foundation for this method.

Key Points

1. Words can take a control over us so that we can't think of anything else.
2. There is nothing wrong with words staying in your head if they are the right words.
3. You need to find some time each day to focus on your goals.
4. It's best to focus on one goal until you act towards it without much effort.
5. You need to focus on your thoughts until it's an unconscious habit.
6. The first thing we need to do is to decide which goal we want to focus on.

Exercises

1. Do you have the time to devote to a goal?

You won't be able to get anywhere near to succeeding without it. How can something be completed if you don't spend any time on it? It's obvious. In exchange for your productive time, you are rewarded. There's no way around. Just imagining that you will be successful without doing anything is deluded.

2. What is the first goal that you want to achieve?

Write it down. Notice I said: the first goal. Not the most important goal. Maybe you just need some confidence in yourself before you tackle the big goals. But of course you may choose your most important goal first. However I would say you should try something that is not too difficult. You have to play some warm up games before you play the championship final.

3. Repeat the following phrase for at least five minutes:

"I deserve <insert the first goal here>"

"I deserve to lose weight."

"I deserve to have love."

"I deserve to be a mother/father."

You do deserve your goal. You deserve anything and everything that you want.

CHAPTER 13. THE FORMULA

I wanted to lose weight. That's a goal many of us have, and if you are lucky to have lost it and reached your target weight, I congratulate you. It's not easy, but it's not impossible. If another person can do it, we can too. How many times have you said to yourself? I want to lose weight. Or another goal. I want more friends. I want happiness. I want a new job. And yet time and time again, nothing happens. I know the feeling. In a dead end job for years. And then having a no growth business for years. Enough. There had to be a time when I said enough. Life has got to change. Have you ever experienced that?

I wanted to lose weight. Yes that's been my goal for years. But I couldn't seem to get anywhere near my target weight. Something had to give for me to change. I think you can guess what. I had a bit of health scare. Not very serious right now. But I understood the consequences. It would be serious if I didn't change.

Do you know what fasting blood glucose is? It's the amount of glucose in your blood after you haven't eaten for a number of hours. To take the test you usually fast overnight, and have some blood taken by your doctor, it's tested and returned. If it's less than 5.6 mmol/L it's considered normal. Between 5.6 and

6.9mmol/L is considered pre-diabetic. And if it's above 7 mmol/L, then it's diabetes.

So I looked at my last blood tests and it said 5.3 mmol/L, in the normal range, but close to the pre-diabetic range. I was thinking maybe that's why I keep putting on weight so easily. My body can't handle sugar very well. So I thought I'd buy a handheld home blood sugar test. I tried it. 5.5 mmol/L. Just below. And I had been eating healthily all week! I thought: "That's not good." So I thought I would test myself on the morning after a good Sunday dinner which was finished off with some delicious cake. I also ate some bread earlier in the day. You can guess what happened. The test read 6.9mmol/L "I knew it!" I thought to myself. I knew something was not correct. I knew that I now must lose weight, and not just weight, but body fat around my stomach.

I want to lose weight, suddenly became, I must lose weight. Do I have a reason to change? Yes! I don't want diabetes. I must lose weight because I don't want diabetes. And this statement encapsulates all that was needed to motivate me to change. It is a goal: losing weight, with a very strong reason for me: I don't want diabetes. Will I eat another piece of cake? No. Not now. Not for a long time. Maybe just on birthdays. Will I eat any other sweets, or bread, or excessive amounts of fruit? No. I must lose weight because I don't want diabetes.

But having a goal and a strong enough reason is not enough to change. It may motivate you for a few days, and then you may get distracted, or you may be too busy, or another crisis occurs. Your original goal is forgotten for the moment. The very strong reason doesn't seem so strong now. Life just does that thing it always does. It shows up, does its thing, and pulls you off course. Then a month has passed and you are no closer to solving your problem, and hopefully, the problem hasn't got worse.

So what do we have to do to so that no matter what happens in life we can stay on track towards our goal? Some things we tend to do without question, and without much thought. Brushing teeth twice a day. It's done everyday without fail. (Well I hope you do!) We learn this as children. But why do we still keep doing it? It's because we keep doing it, and we do it for two minutes. It's hard to forget something you do everyday for at least two minutes twice a day for years upon years of your life. And you don't have to tell yourself that you must brush your teeth because your don't want your teeth to decay.

So the solution is this: You need to be conscious of your goal and strong reason every day without fail, until you no longer have to be conscious of your goal and strong reason. It will become an unbreakable and unshakable part of you. It will be in every fiber of your being.

How will you know that it's now a part of you? You'll feel unease at any time you don't act towards your goal. A day off exercise and you will feel like you can't wait to get back to it. If you are offered a piece of cake you will recoil at the horror of the thought. A day off of planning your day and you will think the whole world will fall apart. It won't. Everything will be fine if you miss a day or two. But it won't feel fine.

And that's the point: you need to create the compulsion in yourself to move towards your goals until you act without fail. If you slept badly, you'll still do it. If you had bad day at work, you'll still do it. If someone says something nasty to you, you'll still do it. Nothing and no-one will stop you.

And in the next chapter I'll describe exactly what you need to do to never forget to act towards your goal. Why should others succeed and not you? There's nothing inherently special about any successful person. It's just that they have behaved differently. Nothing more. You can have everything you want. Never doubt that.

Key Points

1. We have goals that we often don't move towards.
2. Sometimes only a serious event will make us change.
3. A statement can encapsulate all that you need to change.
4. After a few days of making a resolution to change we often forget our goals.
5. We can learn to do things without question and without much thought.
6. You need to be conscious of your goal and strong reason every day without fail, until you no longer have to be conscious of them.
7. You'll feel unease at any time you don't act towards your goal.
8. You need to create the compulsion in yourself to move towards your goals until you act without fail.

Exercises

1. Have you ever had a goal with a strong enough reason?

Write it down. Do you remember how it felt as you changed? Was it difficult? Was it effortless? If it was difficult, why do you believe it was difficult? If it was effortless, why do you think it was effortless? What would you do differently if you had to motivate yourself to reach the goal again?

2. What do you do each day and each week without question?

Write them down. Why do you think you do them without question? What do you think makes you act without hesitation? Do you believe that you can train yourself to do this with other goals?

3. Repeat the following phrase for at least five minutes:

"I can act without hesitation."

By now, you should be able to see the power of these statements repeated to yourself. By themselves, they won't do anything. But they will change the default programming of your mind. You can train yourself to be any way you like.

You can act without hesitation.

CHAPTER 14. THE MAGNIFICENT OBSESSION

Have you ever wanted something so much that you couldn't stop thinking about it? You really wanted a particular type of car, or a particular type of mobile phone? You think about it in the morning and throughout the day. At lunch you may read reviews about the phone. You may think about how it feels in your hand and all the good things you can do with it. On the weekends you may visit a store and see it. You feel it in your hand. You tell yourself you really like it, and you decide at the end of the month to buy it, or you save up the cash and you buy it eventually.

You can also do that with any goal you choose. You can think about it in detail. You can think about how life would be better when you achieve it. You can learn all about how to achieve you goal before you try, which is what I recommend you should do. Maybe you're wondering how you'll find the time to learn. You're already stressed enough as it is. Trust me. When you use this method, you'll find the time.

So let us begin here. Finding time. We need a strong enough reason to find time to focus on a goal. So why do you need to find the time? Why is it so important that no matter what anyone says or does, you must have some time to concentrate on your goals? List the reasons why. And as you list them do you feel very emotional about a particular reason? Do you feel anger, or tears welling up in you? Good. That's your strong reason.

It could be that you want to be the best parent, or the best partner. It could be that you want to buy your own home. Or it could be that you want be your own boss and quit your job. Something has got to power you and that's your strong reasons. I do not want diabetes, that's one of mine. I want to be the best husband that I can be. That's another.

If you don't feel any sort of emotion, then I'd say that you really don't want the goal. Which is perfectly fine. It maybe someone else's goal for you that you really don't want. Your parents want you to be a doctor, but you want to be an entrepreneur. You may feel very strongly at the thought of not becoming a doctor. That's your strong reason. That's what should drive you. The thought of not being told who you should be. It's amazing that there are some parents that still think like that.

Now that we have a strong reason, we can formulate the statement that we will use to summon the unstoppable feeling within us. We are going to create the inability to not act towards our goals. When we combine the goal that we want with the strong reason for the goal we get:

I must <insert goal> because <strong reason>.

I must find the time to focus on my goals because I want to be the best father/mother.
I must find the time to focus on my goals because I want to be a business owner.
I must find the time to focus on my goals because I want to lose weight.

I personally prefer to use a different formulation that flows better when said to oneself:

I must <insert goal> so that I may <strong reason>.

I must find the time to focus on my goals so that I may be the best father/mother.
I must find the time to focus on my goals so that I may be a business owner.
I must find the time to focus on my goals so that I may lose weight.

Now say what you have thought, either within your mind, or out loud. It doesn't need to be said out loud, but doing so may reinforce it in you more. It's your own choice. It will work either way. In fact I don't recommend saying this out loud when you are amongst others. The changes that will come in your life will shock them enough. You don't want them to think you are crazy too.

Say it again. And again. And again. And again for up to thirty minutes. The longer you say it, the faster it will become an unbreakable part of you. After some minutes, you may feel something happening in your body. Your mind will wander the longer you are repeating the statement. Just stop when you realize your mind has wandered, and continue repeating. You don't have to add some extra time if you found your mind wandering.

Now schedule a period of time each day to do this. You can do it in the shower. You can do it whilst traveling on a bus or a train. You can do it at lunchtime at work if you have somewhere where you won't be interrupted. Do it anywhere or at anytime where you won't be interrupted. The more frequently you take some time to repeat the statement, the quicker it will be ingrained you.

I must add one caveat. This works for anything that you want to do. Even bad things. Please don't use it for something that will cause harm to others or yourself. Why would you want to harm yourself or another? You can have anything you want. Why would you want to swap your life for prison life?

This technique is simple and unbelievably powerful. I wish I knew it twenty years ago. There's no point having regrets about the past. Just don't have the same regrets in the future. Better than that, don't let anyone else have the regrets that you yourself had. I hope this technique, along with the exercises in the previous chapters, save you a lot of wasted time, heartache, and pain.

Key Points

1. Sometimes we can't stop thinking about the things we want.
2. We should think about our goals in detail.
3. We need to find a strong enough reason to focus on a goal.
4. You have to feel emotions towards achieving your goals.
5. We can formulate a statement that will create an unstoppable feeling with us.
6. You must continually repeat the statement in your mind as often as possible.
7. The more frequently you take some time to repeat the statement, the quicker it will be ingrained you.

Exercise

Only one exercise: Create your first obsession, and then repeat it to yourself for one week, whenever you can.

POSTSCRIPT

Nothing in the world exists without obsession in some form. Every item you see around you was created by individuals who were obsessed in creating the item. Every man-made event in the world was created by people who obsessed in creating that event. For the majority of time we are just observers of these items and events. We only control what is immediately around us. However we too can guide our thoughts, emotions and obsessions towards whatever we want to create. All the good things that ever existed were created from obsessions. Families. Children. Friendships. Schools. Hospitals. Technology. Democracy. Liberty. Equality. Scientific advancements. None of this could occur without a single-minded focus on it. And then all the bad things that ever existed were created from obsessions. Genocide. Terrorism. War. Abuse. Torture. Slavery. These were all created by humans.

The capacity to be good and bad exists within all of us. If we become obsessed with harmful actions we will act in harmful ways. If we become obsessed with good acts, we will become good people. We will act with kindness, love, and charity to all mankind. We become what we repeatedly think about. I have given you a method to become a truly great person. Please be a good person. Focus on it. Think about it. You are much greater than you think you are. You must believe in your potential. You are so much better than you think you are. You know it. It's within you. The capacity to rise to the occasion. To be greater than you have ever been. Keep stretching yourself and you'll eventually be a giant amongst us. You are limitless. Accept it. Never doubt it.

Paul Shepherd

Email: paul@unstoppablelifenow.com
Website: unstoppablelifenow.com

EXERCISES

The purpose of these exercises is to make you think. It's not enough to simply read a book and hope life will change. If you understand yourself more, you will understand your strengths and weaknesses in more depth. You will be able draw on your experiences to motivate you to change what you want to change. You can choose to do as many as you like in whatever order you like. You may answer a question once, or you may return to it many times.

1. Have you ever mastered a difficult skill at the first attempt? Have you ever needed to try over and over again to get it right? Write down your experience.

2. Do you feel destined for greatness? Have you ever dreamed of a goal that seemed so big that it seemed impossible to achieve? Write it down.

3. Do you procrastinate about doing simple things? Or do you only procrastinate when faced with what you think is a difficult task? Write them down.

4. Do you think it's hard to stop procrastinating? Why?

5. What do you really want but never seems to happen? Why do you think that is so? What do you think is stopping you?

6. Do you prefer trying new and different techniques or do you like just doing the same thing over and over? What do you think is better?

7. Do you want to act when you want and how you want? How would you feel about this? Does it scare you? Does it excite you?

8. Are you tired of trying to improve your life? Would just prefer to just accept life as it is? Or would you never stop until you succeeded?

9. Have you ever changed your attitude to something you really hoped for? Did something you really want turn out to be a big let down?

10. We want the best for ourselves and those we care about. Have you ever felt like you would be unable to provide the best? Does it anger you?

11. Have you ever put on a brave face? Have you ever really wanted life to be much better?

12. Do you like to face up to the truth? Do you prefer to not be aware of all the details? Are you afraid? Or do you prefer to know everything?

13. Do you think you are good enough at a skill and yet you are not successful? Why is that? Do you think that maybe something has to change?

14. Have you ever been in an unacceptable situation? How did it feel? Can you use that emotion to change what you want to change?

15. Do you feel like you are not in control of your life? Do you feel like something or someone else is stopping you?

16. Do you believe that you are responsible for your life? Do you believe that someone else is responsible for your success?

17. Have you ever spent a long time thinking about a mistake of yours that it harmed the lives of the people you cared about?

18. Do you really want to change? Or do you just kind of want to change?

19. Have you been so emotional about some situation that in an instant you changed immediately? Do you think you can recreate that emotional intensity?

20. Do you sometimes do the same thing and expect to have a different result?

21. Do you sometimes expect something to change but you do nothing to make it change?

22. Do you sometimes feel like you are going in the wrong direction towards a goal of yours?

23. Do you think you know the full extent of your capabilities? Could it be possible that you are much greater than you think you are?

24. Have you ever thought that you were not ignoring evidence of your own senses, and then you realized you were wrong later?

25. Do you think you can ignore the results of your actions sometimes? Or do you always think deeply about them?

26. Do you believe that you have to change yourself if you want a new life? Or do you believe that you have to change something external to you?

27. Do you now think about something in a radically different way to how you once thought?

28. Do you believe that someone else is going to change your life? Or do you believe that you can only learn techniques from others?

29. Do you prefer to only learn from your own experiences? Or do you also like to learn from others experiences too?

30. Have you ever thought that you couldn't do anything right? Was it really true?

31. Is there a goal you want, but somehow you don't believe you are capable of achieving it?

32. What can't you stop yourself from doing? Or is it really a struggle to get anything done?

33. Have you ever done something where you did whatever it took to ensure that you would not fail?

34. Have you ever felt like nothing could stop you from succeeding? What did it feel like?

35. If you knew that you would eventually accomplish any goal you chose, what would you choose?

36. Do you know all the things that are necessary to be successful at the goal you desire?

37. Do you know of someone who has achieved the goal that you desire? What can you learn from them?

38. Do you believe you can't acquire the knowledge you need to reach your goals? Why?

39. Do you believe you are not worthy of the goals you desire? Why do you believe that?

40. Do you know anybody that won't support you when you are heading towards your goal?

41. Has anyone ever said to you that your goal is impossible? Did you still act towards it?

42. Do you have the patience to wait for a short period when it appears like nothing is happening?

43. Have you ever succeeded at a goal? And have you ever failed at a goal?

44. Do you believe goals are difficult? Why?

45. Have you ever hesitated acting towards a goal because you believed it was difficult?

46. Have you ever acted easily towards a goal because you believed it was easy?

47. Do you know what prior tasks must be completed before you can achieve your goal?

48. Do you believe your inner voice is just an interpretation of reality? Or do you believe it is an accurate representation of reality?

49. Can you make yourself committed to focus on a particular goal? Does it feel easier now than before?

50. Have you ever succeeded at something whilst being negative? Were you surprised?

51. Have you ever failed at something whilst being positive? What were your thoughts about it?

52. Do you believe that you can't continually break through your comfort zones? Why?

53. Do you believe there is some kind of limit within you stopping you from succeeding?

54. Have you ever done something instantly because you had a strong enough reason to do it?

55. Have you ever felt like failing at a task wouldn't really affect you that much?

56. Have you ever felt uneasy and restless at the thought of not acting towards something?

57. Have you ever tried to motivate yourself by lying to yourself?

58. Do you believe you have self-discipline? Are there times when it doesn't seem to work?

59. Do you often lack self-discipline? What do you believe is the cause of it?

60. Can you instantly turn self-discipline on and off when you need it?

61. Have you ever had a number of competing desires at the same time, but one seemed to have more power than the others?

62. Can you open your mind to the possibility that will-power doesn't exist?

63. Do you keep doing things that you don't want to do?

64. Do you believe you are your thoughts? Why?

65. Has a false thought ever entered your consciousness? What was it?

66. Have you ever had an incorrect memory or interpretation of something? What was it about?

67. Do you believe you can change your interpretations and reactions of events? Why?

68. Can you find some time each day to focus on your goals? When?

69. What goal are you going to focus on first? Write it down.

70. Have you ever wanted something so much that you couldn't stop thinking about it? What was it?

71. Have you thought about your goal in detail? Write down the key details?

72. Do you have a strong enough reason to achieve your goal? What is it?

73. What are the emotions that you feel towards achieving your goal? What are emotions that you would feel if you failed?

74. What is your formulation of the statement described in Chapter 14? Write it down.

75. When will you repeat the statement in your mind? Is it a specific period of time? Or throughout the day?

Made in the USA
San Bernardino, CA
06 September 2019